Puss-in-Boots

Love, Lust, & Treasure

Ravyn Karasu

<u>Abstract</u>

The original *Puss-In-Boots* was written by Charles Perrault in the late 1600's which tells the story of a young man and his clever and manipulative cat working in his favor in return for a pair of boots. In 1979, Angela Carter released her own retelling of the tale under the same title. While Perrault's version follows the familiar formula of fairy tales of the time, Carter decides to take her version on a more adult path with significant differences in certain characters.

A comparison and contrary examination of both texts yield different ideas of both the usage of noun and verb in the themes of lust, love, and treasure. These themes lead the characters to act in accordance to those desires, in some cases, forming their entire character around the premise. In pursuit of these things, we can observe how the characters behave and develop regarding that pursuit. Once these observations have been clearly identified, compared, and contrasted, it can then be observed through the lens of feminist theory. More specifically, we can examine the difference of the modern, or traditional, view of the characters and the woman of desire to that of Carter's post-modern retelling.

Ultimately, we can identify and examine, not just the male pursuits of lust, love, and treasure in their respective stories, but also the female contribution in both the modern and post-modern telling. Therein, we can see the improvement of the feminine presence in Carter's version of the story in contrast to that of Perrault's original telling.

<u>Thesis</u>

❖ ❖

In the world of Angela Carter's *Puss-in-Boots*, Puss, his master, and Signor Panteleone live lives of respective lust and love, and each choose also to treasure, all both in the verbal and objective sense, but the happy ending of the story is the ability of Tabs and Mistress to fulfill *their* love, lust, and claim *their* treasures

<u>The Story & its Variations</u>

❖ ❖

When we hear the name *Puss-in-Boots*, surely, one's imagination first goes to the character in the Dreamworks' franchise, *Shrek*. The most resonant scene is that of his introduction in *Shrek II*, "where he is revealed to be a manipulative little bastard, making his eyes big and cute in order to get what he wants" (Lynley). This sort of behavior is befitting of Puss, as he is a clever character that holds the key to the success of his master. This is true, not only of the modern film adaptations, but of the original version of Charles Parrault and the 1979 rendition by Angela Carter.

When approaching Angela Carter's *Puss-in-Boots*, it is important to note that, not only does she offer a tale through a feminist lens, but that it is also a retelling of a classic fairy tale. While the stories pose happy endings in both instances, Carter offers a more defiant and hopeful finale, which allows the leading female character to swiftly adopt a liberating and brash autonomy of her own wills and desires. To truly understand and appreciate what Carter offers in her rendition, we must examine and familiarize ourselves with the classic from which it draws.

The popular *original* published version of *Puss-in-Boots*, as we generally know it, was penned by 17th century writer Charles Perrault. Perrault is best known for his *Mother Goose* fairy tales, such as, not just *Puss-in-Boots*, but also *Little Red Riding Hood, Cinderella,* and *Sleeping Beauty* (Tolovaj Publishing House). He had written these stories primarily for the entertainment of his own children (Biography). His version of the tale is summarized as follows:

A miller had three sons. On his death bed, he wills his mill to his eldest son, his donkey to his second son, and his cat to his youngest son. Feeling cheated, the youngest son plans to skin and eat the cat. However, Puss convinces him to give him a pair of boots. In return, he plans to help "provide" for his new master.

Once obliged, Puss sets off and hunts rabbits and pheasants and gifts them to the king. These gifts, he claims, are from the **Marquis de Carabas,** *a fictional identity Puss has given his master. While his master is oblivious to the scheme, Puss is still able to provide in unknown favor from the king, as well as the tangible money gifted to him.*

The next step of the plan, Puss learns that the king and princess would be out and about. The master, still oblivious, is convinced to bathe in a river along the designated path of His Majesty's travels. Then, Puss hides his master's clothes and calls in distress to the passing king that thieves have stolen the clothes of the **Marquis de Carabas** as he bathed. The master is quite exposed when the king and his entourage arrive. He is given the king's own spare clothing and a ride. Of course, like any standard fairy tale, he and the princess immediately fall in love with one another.

Puss hasn't finished yet. He rushes ahead to tell (and threaten) the countrymen he finds to, when asked, say that the land belongs to the **Marquis de Carabas**. They do so. Puss then ventures to the castle of an ogre, the true owner of the lands. He tricks the ogre into turning, first, into a mighty lion, then second, into a tiny rat. When the latter occurs, Puss kills and eats him. This leaves the castle open to its new owner, whom of course, Puss proclaims to be the **Marquis de Carabas**. There is already a grand banquet prepared to greet the trio when they arrive. Impressed, the king marries the *princess to the master and Puss is made into a lord. The standard happily-ever-after ensues* (Perrault).

While Perrault is considered the original author, there are, in fact, older versions of the story. These older versions originated from as far east as Russia to as close as Italy. The oldest version didn't even have a cat as the lead role, but a fox (Tolovaj Publishing House). After the so-called happily-ever-after, the fox was killed. In the Italian and Russian versions, the cat, promised a grand funeral after her passing, tests the master's loyalty, only to be thrown out of a window. She runs away in wake of this betrayal, but in the Russian version, she is sure to set the house on fire first (Lynley). Yet, in the Norwegian version of the tale, the master, rather than a miller's son or beggar, is the grandson of the noble who originally owned the lands the ogre has taken for himself. In which case, Puss is returning the birth rite. However, also, in this version, after restoring her master, Puss asks to be beheaded. When this is done, a curse is broken, and she becomes the princess that marries him (Tolovaj Publishing House). It is only with Perrault's version, however, that the cat is explicitly male, and that the boots were introduced.

This then brings us to Carter's modern retelling. In her collection of fairy tales: *The Bloody Chamber*, she has her own version of the tales of Puss and the master. The cat, who calls himself Figaro, is the biased narrator of his own story. To be sure, Carter's rendition is quite the raunchy story, compared to previous versions.

The story opens with Figaro singing his own praises: a master musician, fluent in, not just his own language (Bergamesque, an Italian dialect), but also French, acrobatics, and being an irresistible heart-throb to the ladies (Carter/Grade Saver/Pastos). However, he fails to realize that the "gifts" thrown at him during his performances are meant to silence his terrible yowling. This is how he acquires his boots. Impressed by the cat's reaction to the boots thrown at him, the original owner of said boots takes in the cat as a partner and companion. It is here that Figaro tells of fine bachelorhood debauchery with great glee and fondness.

Everything in their "joyful" dynamic changes when Master lays eyes on the face of a veiled woman and falls madly in love with her, much to Figaro's disappointment. Believing this nonsense can be quelled with good sex, he ventures to the lady's home and prepares to find a way to get them together to do the deed. On this mission, he seduces Mistress' cat, Tabs and learns that Mistress is married to an old, impotent miser named Signor Panteleone, and otherwise in the care of an old hag with an allergy to cats. With this information, the cats make a plan for Master and Mistress to meet.

The first "formal" meeting of Master and Mistress hinges on a rat-catcher hoax. Tabs catches and scatters dead and dying rats about the house. The hag then hires Figaro and Master, disguised as rat-catchers. When brought home, Mistress instructs the hag to leave, to quell her sneezing, while she watches the boys work, "protecting her valuables." Of course, once the hag is gone, Master and Mistress are quick and desperate to come together, with Master taking her virginity. The blood from the encounter is duly blamed on a battle between the cat and a giant rat, of which the hag accepts.

Rather than quell Master's desire, the encounter only fuels his desperate love of her. Figaro is disappointed by this but sets about to make Mistress available for Master to claim as his own. After more meetings with Tabs (both tactical and sexual), a new plan is formed. Master is disguised as a physician this time and hired by the hag once more after Tabs has tripped Signor Panteleone down the stairs, subsequently killing him. The hag is then sent to fetch an undertaker. With her gone and the bed taken, the pair quickly come together for another sexual episode beside the corpse on the floor. They are caught by the hag, but she is fired and paid off as

Mistress declares that she now owns Panteleone's estate and wealth, and that the young man is to be her *new* husband.

The story closes as Figaro realizes that Tabs is pregnant, and the ensuring happily-ever-after is laid out, with Mistress and Master marrying and becoming pregnant, and Figaro and Tabs having a litter of little kittens, topped with a "poetic" closing of Figaro's narrative (Carter, pp.83-103).

Comparison & Symbolism

There is a lot that is similar between Carter and Perrault's version of the tale. There are also notable differences, but also certain aspects met with comparative symbolism, both against each other and in their singular standing. Much of this can be attributed to tradition, rebellion, and the importance of societal rules during the time each story came into being.

For instance, Perrault's story has much of the make-up of the standard fairy tale formula but breaks from these standards as well by removing the damsel in distress factor. In fact, it lacks much to do with the master being heroic in any sense, and places everything upon the cleverness of Puss alone. Contrarywise, we do see a lot of influence of his time within the story and may even explain the purpose of the boots in the story at all.

One must remember that Perrault lived in the 17th century, a time when women were of lesser value to men and seen primarily as chattel for domestic usage and childbearing and rearing (Lynley). It is also important to note the generosity of the miller to his sons. In those times, the inheritance customs would dictate that the eldest son received everything, with any subsequent children having to make their own way (Lynley). As such, the miller managed to split up his estate in a way to make each sibling useful to the whole. The eldest son owned the property and business. The second son owned the donkey that could be used to produce and distribute. While the youngest son seemed worthless, one must remember the value of a good mouser/hunter in the industry of grain. Puss, after all, is an excellent hunter. The path that the miller's youngest son takes shows a level of short-sightedness and his own form of isolation.

Nevertheless, Puss comes to his rescue (time and time again).

"The revelation via the morals dished out by Perrault after the story has ended. [The morality of the story] demonstrates perfectly a double-standard that exists between men and women, in those days as well as these; young men are advised to rely on their own ingenuity rather than upon inherited wealth in order to make their way in the world, whereas young women (or perhaps the men who marry them off as chattel) are advised to question the wealthy young men who come their way, as wealthy appearances do not equal inner goodness, and wealth may be ill-gotten" (Lynley). This can easily be seen in Perrault's story. The princess (or any women for that matter) have nothing to say and are never noted to participate in the conversations therein. The princess might as well have been a lifeless doll for her contribution to the story. He was a good-looking young (naked) man, with which she fell in "love." Indeed, "when the princess first sees the miller's third son, he is naked. Could it not then be believed, that she falls in *lust* with her, rather than falling in *love* with him over his fine clothes" (Interesting Literature)? The more riches he is said to own, both she and the kind grew to love him more and more. The fact that he had so much was what won his favor. That and the cleverness of Puss, which the miller's son simply jelly-fishing his way along.

Of course, we can wonder why Puss would do this. It's obvious that, besides being a cat, Puss is interested in a life of luxury and indulgence and fashion, above his life of toil (Lynley). In order to do this, as he is not a man, he rides along the coat tails of the success he brings his master. Luxury and indulgence make sense, but why fashion? Perrault lived in a time when France was all about the latest fashion. Lynley states that is was not unheard of for families to sell most of what they had, if not their estates, for a good pair of boots or clothing. King Louis XIV of France was about the latest fashion.

One could not enter even enter Versailles without bowing to the grand dress code (Tolovaj Publishing House). The upper class was all about what was worn and by whom. Puss is a gentleman, well-spoken, and seemingly educated. A pair of boots for a cat would have been the first sign of the wealth of the Marquis de Carabas. The man must've had so much wealth, he could afford to boot up his cat. It was an obvious lie, but by the end, it was more than true (through no real effort on the master's part). However, people sure do seem to love stories about the poor underdog.

An interesting fact of note predates Perrault, but plays a potentially interesting link of earlier versions of the tale to Carter's retelling. The earliest version of the story is an Italian piece known as *Panterone* (Interesting Literature). It sounds awfully close to Panteleone. Along this train of thought, we can also link the name Panteleone to its translation, a nickname Figaro gives him: Pantaloon. More specifically, the translation is *pants*, which is considered an ironic name for a man who is neither fit nor virile, but wretched and impotent (Grade Saver). "Panteleone is the stereotyped husband of the 18th century performances, a fool and a miser: Poor, lonely lady, married so young to an old dodder with his bald pate and his goggle eyes and his limp, his avarice, his gore belly, his rheumatics, and his flat all the time at half-mast, and as jealous as he is impotent" (Carter, p.89/Biscala).

Carter also uses the standard formula of the fairy tale that had once been applied and contrasted against Perrault's version. There is no ogre in her story, but there is Panteleone, who very easily could be filling the part of an awful, greedy ogre. The hag is compared to a dragon guarding Mistress' tower and keeping her away from the world outside (Pastos). This is a fair comparison, and it is Figaro and Master that set out to rescue this damsel in distress.

Of course, it's impossible to consider Carter's story without the blatant softcore porn-esque sexuality within and the heavily symbolized role of masculine and feminine power. It is easily seen that Figaro and Master are both very masculine in their behavior. While this changes more drastically in Master, it does so less with Figaro. This can be seen during his rendezvous with Tabs where he believes he is softer, but still displays a deal of chauvinism. He considers the sex he gives Tabs an honor upon her, and he openly narrates the pride he takes in his genitals, which seem to be the *most* prized of his possessions (Grade Saver). The story also offers a suggestion of "female ingenuity and male resentment of it. Stereotypical male response: an inability to show gratitude, or any emotion, in any way other than physical" (Pastos). This can be seen, not just in the sexual contact, but, when faced with Tabs' cleverness, Figaro's gentle bops to head with his paw. "Unlike Figaro, Signor Panteleone is the least sexual but most stereotypically masculine... He represents male power misused to subjugate women" (Grade Saver). It can even be argued that the Mistress' bedroom is like a cocoon of a butterfly. It is in her bedroom where she undergoes both violence and sexual transformation (Pastos). While Master admits his love previous to entering Mistress' bedroom, he still "undergoes a *metamorphosis* in changing his libertine nature for the sake of love. As such, Figaro can be compared to Mr, Lyon's spaniel in Carter's previous story *The Courtship of Mr. Lyon*, wishing his master would turn back into a lion" (Lit Charts). Figaro wishes for his partner of debauchery, misses his role as *valet* and *wingman*. Yet, also, the bedroom is where the "rat-battle" occurs during this meeting between Master and Mistress. It can be noted, when she refers to the fictional rat killed on the sheets as "Puss fighting the biggest beast" is not just a convenient lie, but a lewd code for her virginal parts dealing with Master's penis (Biscala).

Another thing to note is the symbolism of the transference of power. Signor Panteleone has a large ring of keys. Every key goes to something of value to him, including his riches, his properties, and including the key to the bedroom of his wife most likely. Mistress "is a bold and vibrant person, only pacified by the fear of her husband" (Grade Saver). However, the key ring "is a symbol of power changing hands. Mistress is now an officially empowered woman" once she takes the key ring from Panteleone's corpse (Biscala).

One can even see the difference in the role of the female characters in both Perrault and Carter's versions. As previously stated, the princess says nothing, or is never acknowledged as saying anything in Perrault's version of the story. In Carter's story, we see that women are speaking, but the attention to dialogue is subjugated to second-handedness. The hag is often relegated to this position, as she is not a *person* but a *thing* that is in the story. After Master's first sexual encounter with Mistress, she suddenly has a voice. Her dialogue is marked by quotation marks. She has her *own* voice. However, we can see that, even with his domestication, Figaro is still chauvinistic over the voice of his clever Tabs. She has proven herself throughout the entire affair, yet she never gains her own voice. She is subjugated to the second-handed voice Figaro narrates. He may love her, but he still sees her as less important than himself (Pastos).

Love, Lust, & Treasure: Property & Agency

Earlier, we discussed the role of women during 17th century France, when Perrault would have written his fairy tale. Women were seen as inferior to men, were seen as chattel or domestic appliances, more or less. We can also see how, with the absence of the princess uttering a single word, that even she was simply a commodity with which to barter. The king's lands would merge with the *Marquis de Carabas'* with the marriage of the princess to him. This was the traditional way things were and are considered the standard for the creation of a traditional fairy tale.

When Carter tells her version of *Puss-in-Boots*, it's less a standardized notion and more of an obnoxious and highlighted reality of the Italian town in which the story occurs. Mistress was not a human being. She was property and a victim of female objectification. She was made to wear a veil when she attended church and was to always be accompanied by her keeper (the hag). Also, she was allowed to only look out of her tower window for one hour ever night with the express order to never smile while doing so (Grade Saver/Pastos). "Signor Panteleone is a miser with all of his possessions, including his young wife. Because he sees her as property, he feels justified in keeping her locked up" (Grade Saver). It is clear that the townsfolk either don't know or don't care about her treatment. "They [the townsfolk] do not help the miserable young woman in their midst because they find it acceptable for a man to control his wife. The young woman…is imprisoned literally in the hose, but more importantly, she is a prisoner of chauvinism" (Grade Saver). It can only be assumed, through Mistress' fear and dislike of her husband, that she was likely forced to marry him for economic and/or social gain

(Grade Saver). Then again, this was the norm throughout most of history.

Within the story, Panteleone's greed (lust for possessions), eagerness to treasure (objects, of which his wife is one), and his impotence culminate into a horrid display of behaviors and thoughts that lack any sort of mutuality. "Tabby declares—he'd put a stop to all the rutting in the world, if he had his way, just to certify his young wife don't get from another what she can't get from him" (Carter, p.89). Later, she tells Figaro "Another draught of Adam's ale healthfully concludes the day; up he tucks besides Missus and, since she is his prize possessions, consents to finger her a little. He palpitates her hide and slaps her flanks: 'What a good bargain!' Alack, can do no more, not wishing to profligate his natural essence. And so drifts off to sinless slumber amid the prospects of tomorrow's gold" (Carter, p.99). Carter's dictation of words such as *hide*, *flank*, and *bargain* make it painfully clear that he sees his wife as sub-human (Grade Saver). These are the sorts of terms used for the purchase of a fine horse.

It is after the death of Mistress' husband that we see the true culmination of her liberation. She not only grows due to a mutual sexual relationship, but then becomes quite a bold figure and claims her new power and freedom with gusto. Master does not seek to rule over her but is content to be happy with her. Even Figaro realizes the importance of a mutual relationship when he concludes "So may all your wives, if you need them…" and "all your husbands, if you want them," making it clear that both genders have a choice in the matter, or should (Carter, p.109). This certainly makes Carter's version of the story more open to modern feminist ideals about a woman's agency.

<u>Morality</u>

There's no question that, unlike *Aesop's Tales*, or more traditional fairy tales, *Puss-in-Boots* doesn't present a clear moral, and the morality present within is potentially condemnable on the surface. For Perrault's version, one can only assume the moral is something like "Don't waste your time complaining. The cards are in your hands. If you play them right, you will be rewarded" (Tolovaj Publishing House). It can also be that one should have "good manners, good looks, and good dress" in order to succeed (Tolovaj Publishing House). Of course, this doesn't offer much hope to anyone who is born—less attractive.

In contrast, while the moral is still not entirely clear, it is easier to draw *something* from it. "Morality is undoubtedly complicated because deceit, adultery, and murder are necessary in order for sexual mutuality to triumph over sexual subjugation" (Grade Sever). With such a bold statement, one must wonder if it applies simply to the story, or if this is a fundamental feminist call-to-arms. Let's hope it is the former.

All this being said, we can also, perhaps, deduce that Perrault's *Puss-in-Boots* had no grand parable of morality, but was meant to simply be enjoyed. He did write them for his children, after all. Unlike his other tales, *Puss-in-Boots* doesn't offer any elegance like *Cinderella* or *Sleeping Beauty*, both stories in which the female leads do practically nothing and come out as successes. This, of course, would depend on which version is read, as both *Cinderella* and *Sleeping Beauty* have some rather dark connotations and actions, as well as evilly satisfying endings. *Little Red Riding Hood* could be argued to have a more active lead role, but a clearer moral of perhaps "don't talk to strangers" and the like. For

Puss-in-Boots, the story comes off as a rascal tale, with Puss doing ultimately for himself and his master being a useless pawn for his scheme.

For Carter's version, while the story is still rather masculine, with Figaro being the narrator and retaining chauvinistic views, though still somewhat domesticated, we can see communication between all the parties for whom we are supposed to cheer. Everyone, from Figaro, to Master, to Mistress, and to Tabs all do *something* to further venture towards what they want. All of them have to be clever in order to get somewhere. For Mistress, it was her liberation. For Master, it was Mistress' love. For Tabs, it was for the happiness of Mistress and her desire to please Figaro. For Figaro, he did it for the happiness of his master. All of the important characters have both a guilty and innocent motive to exist in the story. For a modern retelling, Carter's *Puss-in-Boots* offers the most profound moral/advice. It's not so much the negatives to achieve a positive, as one source suggests.

A modern commentary is necessary to truly appreciate the subtle moral of the 1979 tale. Of course, one must recognize that the Bergamo setting is likely a time long before 1979 and its progressive ideals that were going into practice. Women were still subject to their husbands, whereas Carter's world was seeing a shift in agency of young women going out into the world, able to exist without the lording of fathers and husbands. The comfort of women growing up to experience these wonders is subtly evident in Carter's tale. Women were finding their voice, and as Mistress came out from beneath the lording of her husband, and began to exist for herself, she gained her own voice, and it culminated in her defiance of the traditional subservient wife and gave rise to a woman who could explore what she wanted and to feel loved in a way that was mutually pleasing and equal.

It is also important to see the shift of the main characters of both versions (Perrault's miller's son and Carter's rogue bachelor) and their investment to their success. As stated, with Perrault's other fairy tales, *Cinderella* and *Sleeping Beauty* specifically, there is an element of "wait for the man." The key to success was to wait for the man. Perrault doesn't even give the princess enough personality to acceptably apply "wait" to her. Instead, it is the miller's youngest son that waits for things to be handed to him. He does absolutely nothing to invest in his own success. It's no wonder he showed such a lack of gratitude in older versions of the tale pre-dating Perrault. He didn't have to contribute to his own success. Perhaps, this is why older versions added Puss' resentful curse at the end: "Once a beggar, always a beggar" in response to his betrayal of her (Tolovaj Publishing House).

Contrary to Perrault, Carter's characters are all active in their own success. There is a great deal of active cooperation and communication between all four of the important parties. As such, it makes Carter's tale a more satisfying one, as we are put in a position to care about the characters and hope that their investments and actions are not in vain. Figaro still tells Master what to do, but unlike with Perrault's tale, Master is aware of what is being done and why. We can care about his motives because *he* cares about his motives, unlike with the miller's son, where he didn't seem to care one way or another. In essence, the greatest moral one can find for Carter's *Puss-in-Boots*, is the notion to know what you want and *do* something to *invest* yourself. Contribute to your own success rather than waiting for someone else to give it to you without any work put in from oneself.

<u>Conclusion</u>
❧ ❧

Puss-in-Boots is a fun and memorable story. Even today, it is being told and retold, and the character of Puss is as popular as ever. We can enjoy a Spanish-flavored rendition with William Shatner as the titular cat, or we can enjoy the antics of Puss in the infamous *Shrek* films. Funnily enough, the William Shatner dub of *Puss-in-Boots* feels more akin to the original Perrault tale, as it uses Perrault's layout primarily. Whereas, the Dreamworks' rendition of Puss feels much more akin to that of Carter's version, as he is a seductive orange cat: clever, acrobatic, and a stud among the ladies.

In a world that is pushing for more feminist progressiveness, it's not unreasonable to see the retellings of this tale become saturated with more strong and active female support characters seeking their own agency. Regardless of how it ages, there's always something *different* about it and its formula compared to that of other fairy tales. As time goes on, we'll likely see the story undergo more changes and become even more relatable to its audiences. We already see this in Dreamworks' rendition of the title, where the titular character went from a side character in one movie to the focus of his own. However, the film has totally deviated from the original fairy tale presented by either Perrault or Carter, yet still entertains adults and children alike and offers a new set of morals and social commentary. However, be it Perrault, Carter, or any modern addition to the legacy of *Puss-in-Boots*, there will always be some allusion towards the concepts of love, lust, and treasure.

<u>Works Cited</u>

❖ ❖

Biography. "Biography-Charles Perrault." *Biography*, A&E Television Networks, 2 Apr. 2014, www.biography.com/people/charles-perrault-9438047. Accessed 4 Nov. 2018.

Biscala, Marla. "Angela Carter's «Puss-in-Boots»: Commedia Dell'arte Meets the Bluebeard Story | Request PDF." *ResearchGate*, 1 Jan. 2004, www.researchgate.net/publication/277200114_Angela_Carter's_Puss-in-Boots_Commedia_dell'arte_meets_the_Bluebeard_story. Accessed 26 Oct. 2018.

Carter, Angela. "Puss-in-Boots." *The Bloody Chamber*, Penguin Books, 1979, pp. 83-103.

GradeSaver. "The Bloody Chamber "Puss-in-Boots" Summary and Analysis." *Study Guides & Essay Editing | GradeSaver*, 22 Oct. 2015, www.gradesaver.com/the-bloody-chamber/study-guide/summary-puss-in-boots. Accessed 26 Oct. 2018.

Interesting Literature. "A Summary and Analysis of the 'Puss in Boots? Fairy Tale." *Interesting Literature*, 14 Oct. 2017, interestingliterature.com/2017/10/19/a-summary-and-analysis-of-the-puss-in-boots-fairy-tale/. Accessed 29 Oct. 2018.

LitCharts. "The Bloody Chamber Puss-in-Boots Summary & Analysis from The Creators of SparkNotes." *LitCharts*, 2018, www.litcharts.com/lit/the-bloody-chamber/puss-in-boots. Accessed 26 Oct. 2018.

Lynley. "Puss In Boots by Charles Perrault." *Slap Happy Larry*, 16 June 2017, www.slaphappylarry.com/short-story-study-puss-in-boots-by-charles-perrault/. Accessed 29 Oct. 2018.

Pastos, Georgia. "Puss in Boots (The Bloody Chamber) Analysis." *Academia.edu - Share Research*, 2018, www.academia.edu/12267541/Puss_in_Boots_T he_Bloody_Chamber_Analysis. Accessed 26 Oct. 2018.

Perrault, Charles. "SurLaLune Fairy Tales: The Annotated Puss in Boots." *SurLaLune Fairy Tales: Annotated Fairy Tales, Fairy Tale Books and Illustrations,* 29 July 2013, www.surlalunefairytales.com/pussboots/index.html. Accessed 25 Oct. 2018.

Tolovaj Publishing House. "Puss in Boots: A Story With a Questionable Moral." *Owlcation,* 21 Sept. 2012, owlcation.com/humanities/puss_in_boots. Accessed 29 Oct. 2018.